# SMALL BEGINNINGS: A COLLECTION OF POEMS

I0201915

A catalogue record for this book is available from the National Library of Australia

Published 2022

ISBN: 978-0-6453762-7-2 (epub)
ISBN: 978-0-6453762-8-9 (paperback)
ISBN: 978-0-6453762-9-6 (hardcover)

9 780645 376289

Published with the aid of Jumble Books and Publishers (https://jumblebooksandpublishers.com).

# Image Credits:

Hannah (aged 16), Blackpool, 15 September 1932.

Freesia detail by Brigid Morrigan.
(Freesias were Hannah's favourite flowers.)

# Small Beginnings

## A Collection of Poems

by

Hannah Entwistle

# Contents

# Foreword

Hannah Bristo was born in Cumbria just south of the Scottish border in England. She moved to Lancashire when young and worked in a textile mill in the time after the First World War.

Hannah met and married my grandfather, Wilton Entwistle, and settled in a tiny town on the out skirts of Bolton, called Westhoughton, which is where she lived out the years of raising children.

As a child, I went to visit my grandparents often at their cosy house, enjoying the produce my grandfather grew in his garden (he was an avid gardener and his garden had the air of an allotment or market garden with the volume of produce that he grew). My grandmother would bake standing at an old green painted dresser with a fold-down table and I would stand next to her on a small stool watching her make blackcurrant puddings, economical macaroons and many other sweet and savoury morsels. Eventually, my grandparents moved to a small house in a seaside town in north Wales called Rhyl and it was there she lived the last decades of her life.

Hannah captured her unique view of the world in a series of poems she penned throughout her life and my mother thought to capture and keep the collection as an heirloom of our family's history. I was most insistent that these thoughts and musings would not be forgotten and am honoured and pleased to be able to collect them into this work. My mother will cry when I show her, I am sure.

Brigid Morrigan
February 2022

# Look Around

Look at things clearly, open your eyes wide.
View everything differently, sweep the cobwebs aside.

There are lots of pleasant things, everywhere to be seen.
Don't waste your time walking about in a dream.

You can always find beauty in everyday things.
The fragrance of a garden, what pleasure that brings.

The clean freshness of a wind. The coolness of rain.
How would we feel, never to experience it again?

Hear the music of laughter, from a contented baby.
The call of a bird, wooing his mate, maybe?

The rustle of leaves, in a gentle cool breeze.
Free for everyone, the pleasure of these.

See the sky at night, a curtain of velvet.
Sprinkled with stars, like a heavenly pelmet.

Stained with red, a shepherd's delight.
Heralding good weather, sunshine so bright.

See a harvester working in a waving cornfield.
Mother Nature's gift, a bounteous golden yield.

Everywhere around us, is beauty of some kind.
To be seen clearly, if cobwebs we sweep from the mind.

# Nature

Isn't nature a truly wonderful and marvellous thing?
Plant one tiny seed and see the pleasure it will bring.

Look after it well and treat it the right way.
It responds to a pep talk, so some people say.

It's a miracle watching a plant's leaves unfold.
Nature really is a wondrous sight to behold.

In nature's garden, flaws are very few.
Beautiful scented blooms grow, in every kind of hue.

Think of the pleasure gained from one tiny seed.
A little of God's earth is all they really need.

Cuttings you can take, and so it goes on.
You end up with lots of plants, all from just one.

All the plant asks is a little care from you.
A drink now and then, that's not hard to do.

Plant's don't go on strike. Don't need any wages.
They don't vandalise things or fly into rages.

Given right conditions they grow day by day.
We could learn quite a lot from nature's way.

From an acorn a mighty oak tree can grow.
Lots of things come from small beginnings you know.

# Reminiscing

Sitting around the fire chatting as folks sometimes do.
Reminiscing and telling stories, some false and some true.

The talk veered around to when they were young.
Of things they had seen, and what they had done.

One man lighting his pipe, puffed out a cloud of smoke.
Said, 'I'll tell you a true tale about me and another bloke.

'Tommy was a weedy, poor looking lad, a bit younger than me.
Folks thought him a bit slow, and made fun of him you see.

'I was off to Wembley one year and promised to take him along.
I just hoped he'd stick by me and not get lost in the throng.

'I remembered it well. We travelled down overnight.
We were in London long before it was daylight.

'We trudged around looking for somewhere to eat.
Finding a café, we went in and took the weight off our feet.

'Tommy was excited; it was his first time in London town.
And could hardly wait, to have a look around.

'We weren't due at the match till just after one.
So we'd have a few hours for some sightseeing to be done.

'Buckingham Palace we both thought was a must.
So off we went, thinking we'd start there first.

'Outside a tall building was a crowd looking up horrified.
The place was on fire, with two children inside.

'Smoke was pouring out of the windows, and screams we could hear.
A spectator said, "The brigade was on the way, but might be too late I fear.

'"We've done our best to save them, been beaten back by the heat.
It's terrible to feel so helpless, fire is a devil to beat."

'Turning to speak to Tommy, I realised he wasn't there.
He'd gone into that inferno, to try to rescue the pair.

'After a time he appeared at the window holding a boy and a babe.
The fire engine arrived, now hopefully they'd be saved.

'A ladder was raised; it seemed such a long way to climb.
The fire was burning so fiercely, please God they'd be on time.

'With bated breath we watched that dreadful scene.
As tongues of flame licked the window where Tommy was last seen.

'Then a might cheer went up, as thro' the smoke two men came in sight.
Clinging to the ladder, each with a child clutched tight.

'Another few minutes really would have been too late.
And quite a different tale I'd now have to relate.

'I was glad to see Tommy. My relief was immense.
For even from across the road, the heat was intense.

'They handed the terrified kids to their weeping, grateful Mum.
Who chokingly said "God bless you lads for saving my daughter and son."

'Then while attention was centred on the kids and their Mum
We walked off down the road, in the direction we had come.

'Walking towards Wembley, we were soon swallowed up by
the crowd.
"Anyone could have done it," said Tommy, not a bit proud.

'His clothes were singed, and so was his hair.
But, after a wash and brush up, he looked pretty fair.

'We went to the match, with no sign that he was in pain.
Till we were going home again, and back on the train.

'He showed me his hands all blistered and red.
"I couldn't spoil the match for you," he quietly said.

'We were a bit downhearted as out team hadn't won.
The doctor at the infirmary, asked how the burns had been
done.

'But Tommy swore me to secrecy, wouldn't let me tell.
He'd had a dizzy turn, he said, and on the fire he had fell.

'It happened a few years ago, to tell now won't matter.
Tommy made up in heart what he lacked in stature.

'It just goes to show big hefty lads aren't always the best.
Little plucky ones can their own when put to the test.'

## Father Time

Try keeping a check on Old Father Time.
After all these years he's still in his prime.

He's someone no one can completely ignore.
Time is always there, right at the fore.

Hurry! Hurry! We say time is a-wasting.
But minutes that are gone we can't be replacing.

Time never stands still. It ticks mercilessly on.
Before we know it there's another hour gone.

Old Father Time is a stern taskmaster.
When enjoying oneself he makes time go faster.

But try doing something you just hate to do.
Then time seems to stand still, just to spite you.

Each minute that goes by, you can never recapture.
We think we can, when it's recalled a short time after.

But minutes can only be lived one at a time.
So make each one count then all will be fine.

Live life to the full. Enjoy those fleeting hours.
Don't waste precious time bemoaning the showers.

Look for the sunshine that follows the rain.
For time marches on, too quick once again.

## Brush Mania

Some work keeps the hands busy, but not the mind.
Thoughts wander back and forth, least that's what I find.

Have you ever thought how many brushes there are?
There's shoe brushes, clothes brushes, even one for the car.

Long brushes, hand brushes and paint brushes too.
There's even a special one for cleaning the loo.

Tooth brushes, to keep our teeth sparkling bright.
That's the one we use before bed every night.

Hair brushes to use on our crowning glory.
One hundred strokes a day, or is that an old story?

Pastry brushes to put a glaze on a tart.
Make up brushes, which create a work of art.

Flue brushes, nail brushes, and one to clean drains.
Long handled ones, to clean windows without any strains.

There are scrubbing brushes and suede brushes too.
Hat brushes, hearth brushes, to name but a few.

There's a brush for every job, so it would seem.
You can even use one to sweep away a dream.

It's common knowledge that a fox has a brush.
While a brush with the law, is kept very hush hush.

No skill needed in using a sweeping brush, so people say.
But remember, no one likes to be brushed the wrong way.

## Our Little Pal

One winter's day Hubby said 'Come and see what I've got.'
It was a dear little puppy, so small; he would fit into a teapot.

A lovely little corgi, greeted with lots of jollity.
He couldn't have been better loved, if he'd belonged to royalty.

Eventually he was house trained and really very good.
Taking me for daily walks, in the nearby leafy wood.

Lots of pleasure he gave us, with his funny little ways.
Doing his best to comfort me, if I had one of those black days.

If we had to leave him for just a little while.
The welcome was marvellous, done in doggy style.

He gave us 14 years of love and loyal devotion.
Small wonder when he went, we was overcome with emotion.

There could never be another to fill that empty place.
We will never forget our Sandy with his lovely expressive face.

## A Prayer of Thanks

Thank you God, for the small everyday things.
The joy and pleasure these small things bring.

Waking in the morning, to a bright new day.
Being able to hear what other people say.

To see the sun shining thro' the trees.
We sometimes forget to thank you for these.

Yet, what a difference to our lives, these small things make.
But often for granted, these blessings we take.

# Fate

Who can tell what lies in store, as we journey on life's way.
Taking the rough with the smooth and living day by day.

Sometimes it seems the bad days outnumber all the rest.
The only thing we can do is to do our best.

Dealing with whatever comes along, on each recurring day.
In moments of stress, everyone reacts in a totally different
way

Courage is born of determination and grit.
When there are jobs to be done, you just get on with it.

To some it's challenging, brings out their best.
While others can't cope, they crumble when put to the test.

Trouble drives some, to the very brink of despair.
Acting on impulse, they just don't seem to care.

Then like some vandals, go off on the rampage.
To ease their frustration and work off their rage.

But blindly rush in, where angels fear to tread.
Afterwards, regretting a lot that's been said.

While others bottle it u p and imagination runs riot.
Worrying, sometimes needlessly, and keeping very quiet.

Who can tell just which way is the best.
Or how each one will react, when put to the test.

## Life's Ups and Downs

Never give up so how hard the way.
There's light at the end of the tunnel they say.

It's good to have a friend ready with a helping hand.
Someone always there, who tries to understand.

Carry on the fight. Don't despair.
Take one day at a time and you will get there.

Don't give in at the first set back.
Show that it's stamina, which you don't lack.

Keep a stiff upper lip whatever folks say.
You are sure to win thro at the end of the day.

Don't let life's hard knocks get you down.
Meet them half way with a grin, not a frown.

Then before you know it, life's back on an even keel.
A lot stronger and better, that's what you will feel.

You can't expect sun all of the time.
Everyone has rough patches, not all sunshine.

It's how you face them that shows the real you.
Hold your head high and you're bound to come thro.

Take heart, you know, you're never alone.
God watches us all from his heavenly home.

## Memories

A friend and I planned a holiday by the sea.
Off we went to Llandudno to see how that would be.

A hotel on the front was where we planned to stay.
We just couldn't wait to start our holiday.

But the sun decided to go away that week too.
We weren't bothered with lots of things to do.

We showered each morning, before a walk on the prom.
Back in time for breakfast, a tonic for any one.

We climbed the Orme discovering new paths and ways.
Feeling muscles we didn't know we had until the next day.

We have had a 'Jacuzzi' one afternoon for fun.
The cleanest holidaymakers in Llandudno, by gum.

We had fun in the silliest funny ways.
Relaxed and happy we were, our worries far away.

We must have walked miles on our outings out there.
Nothing compares with a walk in the lovely fresh air.

There are lots of seats, a godsent to poor walkers like us.
On going to places inaccessible by bus.

We walked and exercises and returned full of beans.
So a holiday without sun does one good so it seems.

## Reflections from a Hospital Bed

Lying in hospital, with both eyes bandaged tight.
Thoughts fly about at random, likes swallows in full flight.

Hearing tends to sharpen, noise takes on a new meaning.
Fitting faceless voices to people, takes quite a lot of reasoning.

Eating becomes quite tricky, when one's plate one can't see.
Things we take for granted, not at all as it should be.

Thank God it was only temporary, not like the permanent blind.
They are the ones whom I admire, courageous too I find.

It's easy for sighted people to roam about at will.
But to the blind, who are in darkness, it must be a bitter pill.

To miss the rainbow colours, live in a permanent black, dark state.
And yet, be cheerful as they are, not rant and rail at life's hard fate.

To miss the ordinary things, we all take for granted still.
Imagine not to see the sky, or heather on a hill.

To accept God's will so bravely, carry on just the same.
Exceptional people they must be, no pity do they claim.

Characters are found by hardships, and endured day by day.
A pity some must find life's highway up hill all the way.

## Spring Spring

Spring is here when birds start nesting.
So patient they sit, endurance testing.

Showing Mother love at its very best
Nature's way puts love to the test.

Soon chick will hatch, making Mother so proud.
She's soon busy feeding and guarding her little crowd.

Teaching each one to fly, soon they'll flee the nest.
Mother so happy, has passed nature's test.

Without nature's wonders, a poor world it would be.
No birds to sing, no flowers to see.

Never to feel the rain on one's face.
Without trees the world would be a very bare place.

None so blind as those who can't see.
They kill the birds, and mutilate the tree.

Nothing but ugly manmade buildings will be left soon.
Roads, and cities, no beauty, nature they doom.

## That Elusive Name

You must agree memory is a tricky thing.
Forget something then your troubles begin.

Try to remember somebody of fame.
You recall the face, but what was the name?

Just like a dog with a juicy marrowbone.
You have got to go on, can't leave it alone.

You *have* to know, it becomes a test.
You worry and think, it gives you no rest.

You think and puzzle, but to no avail.
You just can't remember that elusive male.

'till in exasperation, you say, 'Bother the man.'
Whatever his name, it doesn't matter a damn.

Even if you remember, it's really no gain.
So why worry and tease your poor old brain.

It's not really important, it's just you lack.
That bit of memory, when thinking back.

Your memory is rust, it plays tricks on you.
Just one of the things old age can do.

Then all at once, right out of the blue.
The name just happens to come to you.

## If Only

If only we'd known, and now it's too late.
Heartaches are caused when promises we break.

If only we'd realised how much is meant.
To reply to the letter which someone sent.

If only we hadn't been so easily led.
Believing everything someone had said.

If only we hadn't rushed blindly on.
Saying all sorts of things we shouldn't have done.

If only we knew the right words to say.
To right the wrongs, take the pain away.

If only, if after the vent, words so easy to say.
But the saddest words used in the world today.

## Happy Thoughts

When you are happy things look bright and gay.
Life seems more worthwhile living every day.

We all wish for happiness in our short lives.
For that little something, which everyone strives.

It means something different to everyone.
What pleases one does nothing for some.

Happiness affects people in many different ways.
And seems to be altered, with the moon's every phase.

Whatever it is that triggers it off, for you.
I hope that elusive happiness visits you too.

## The Party

Dolly's parents were away for a long weekend.
'I'll have a party,' she thought, so rang up her friends.

'We'll have sandwiches and cakes, and I'll make a meat pie.'
She hadn't made pastry before, but thought she would try.

She also tried cakes, but didn't do too well.
She didn't get it right as every one fell.

Some resembled doughnuts, with a hole in the middle.
While others looked like drop scones, cooked on a griddle.

Any way she filled up the hollows with icing in pink.
Optimistically telling herself, 'They'll be alright, I think.'

Busy with the icing, she clean forgot about the pie.
Still in the oven, it was now black and dry.

Well that's no good, any body can see.
Even the dog refused it when offered it for tea.

She slashed her finger while cutting the bread.
So gave up, and dashed out for a sliced loaf instead.

She concocted all sorts of fancy pate's and spreads.
Then made a tall pyramid of brown and white bread.

Filling a bowl with potato crisps ready salted.
At least these can't possibly be faulted.

But turning quickly she walked into an open door.
Smash went the bowl, and crisps all over the floor.

Crunching over the crisps and rubbing her head.
This blooming party, she was beginning to dread.

With a lump on her head, and on her finger a plaster.
She tried to salvage order out of the disaster.

Crisps and glass bowl thrown out in the bin.
Along with the meat pies, complete with Mum's pie tin.

Surely, nothing else could go wrong with her day.
She could have cried with vexation as she put the brush away.

Rushing to open the door, she slipped on the mat.
Her guests didn't expected to be greeted like that.

On her hands and knees, and in curlers and pinny.
What a start to her party, she felt like a ninny.

She had so wanted everything to go just right.
But it all had gone wrong, now she looked a sight.

Her guests were early, all looked very smart.
So she welcomed them in with a drink for a start.

She rushed upstairs but she didn't take much care.
When removing her curlers and combing her hair.

A bottle of perfume spilled over her dress, what a pong.
How they laughed when told of all that had gone wrong.

From a very poor start the party went with a swing.
Surprising what cheeriness a few drinks will bring.

They all enjoyed themselves, agreeing Dolly had done fine.
But she'll remember her first party for a very long time.

## Spring At Last

Spring is on its way at last, I think.
Crocus and Daffodils are on the brink.

Almost bursting right out of their shell.
Spring exuberance, nothing can quell.

Soon, hundreds of Daffodils will dance in the breeze.
Like a golden carpet spread out under the trees.

Horrid, cold winter, just a memory will be.
Mother Earth will wake and the flowers will be free.

Daffodils nodding their lovely trumpety heads.
Calling all the other flowers, 'Get out of bed.'

Tulips answer the call, they won't be long I know.
Aubrietia and Forget-me-nots will be next to show.

Soon Roses will be here, in every kind of hue.
They really are so lovely; a song of praise is due.

To a real old English garden, there's nothing to compare.
What would the world be like, without a garden fair.

To wander in a garden, or just to stand and stare.
Beauty is there for everyone, all of us to share.

All the work we do is repaid by a lovely show.
Pleasure and satisfaction, when the seeds we planted grow.

## Wishes

Of washing up, making beds etc, I am so sick.
I think in my next life, something else I will pick.

Maybe as a cat and do nothing all day, just play with a ball.
But, being put out at night, I wouldn't like that at all.

Perhaps I'll be a horse, and in the meadows I'll play.
But then I could be a carthorse, and have to work all day.

How about being a bird, flying high and free.
Ugh! I don't fancy eating worms for breakfast, lunch and tea.

Stuck out in all weathers, with head tucked under wing.
It's not a very joyful life; I wonder why they all sing?

To be a squirrel, flitting from tree to tree.
And hibernate all winter, how lovely that would be.

But not so nice worrying about being skinned.
Because some one wants a coat collar trimmed.

Utopia must only exists in one's mind.
There are drawbacks in everything, I find.

So content with my lot, I must try to be.
For it's not <u>always</u> bad just to be me.

## Our Varied Weather

Old Mr. Weather has many changeable moods.
Very cold, or snowing, with a few mild interludes.

Even when predicted, it's not always as they say.
Atmospheric conditions vary such a lot, changing every day.

Blowing a gale the wind never seems to rest.
Not a bit of wonder our hearths are put to the test.

We can't rely on the weather, everyone says.
Never quite the same on two consecutive days.

Secretly we're hoping for a lovely warm mild spring.
We will have to just accept whatever he chooses to bring.

What an old disgruntled fellow, Mr. Weatherman must be.
Come on buck up, wake up Mr. Sun, that's who we want to
see.

We are tired of huddling round the fire, trying to keep warm.
Wondering if precious plants outside, are weathering the
storm.

So just take advantage of any nice sunny warm days.
But keep our coats handy whatever the weatherman says.

## The Pattern of Life

The patchwork quilt looked very gay.
A kaleidoscope of colour in every way.

Like life, showing the pattern of the days.
Bright and sunny ones, interlaced with hose of grey.

Life isn't made up of <u>all</u> happy times.
It fluctuates without reason or rhyme.

Characters are built from life's intricate patterns.
Some strong, some broken, but some are just flattened.

Ready to spring up as they pattern is changed.
But like the quilt, each piece is pre-arranged.

All slotted into a place, ever so gay.
Taking in the bright and the dull, on its way.

Patches of colour delicately matched.
Shades arranged so no two will clash.

Sprinkled all over with a glittering shower.
Showing the presence of a divine power.

Fashioned and styled by loving hands.
Woven by destiny in life's golden strands.

## A Cold in the 'Dose'

When you've got a cold and are feeling quite dense.
Don't you sometimes wish your nose were somewhere else?

Thought fly thro my mind, as to <u>just</u> where.
The thing could go, if it wasn't put there.

If on top of the head, might interfere with one's hat.
Then if one sneezed, just think of that.

Hats would go flying all over the street.
Causing chaos, by getting under folks' feet.

It wouldn't do at all, if put at the back of the head.
Might be a bit awkward when lying in bed.

Really on the whole, it's perhaps in the best place.
It's the nose, after all, which gives character to the face.

Every one looking alike, and we wouldn't want that!!!
Without one, faces would look very flat.

Perhaps it's really better, to put up with it.
Even when like a beacon, and it sometimes is lit.

Usually, most noses aren't that bad.
No use to complain, it's the only one we have.

## A Slimmer's Dilemma

I wonder why we women try to keep slim.
Trying to keep our figures ever so trim.

Men don't seem to worry, they bulge here and there.
In places we women just wouldn't dare.

My weight has gone up, I'm very sad.
I've lost the figure that I once <u>nearly</u> had.

I'll start slimming again, but not today.
Tomorrow's the best time to start, they always say.

Before summer I really must get into trim.
But I just can't bring myself to begin.

My will power is at a very low ebb.
In fact, I can almost say that it's dead.

But try to do something I really must.
If all my clothes I don't want to bust.

My case in fact, is getting quite urgent.
Wonder if I should scrub myself with detergent?

Perhaps that's a bit drastic, maybe even silly.
Don't wish to be skinless, must a bit skinny.

I mustn't eat spuds or biscuits or cake.
And try my best, to not test what I bake.

A nudist maybe, I might have to be.
All the clothes that I have won't fit me.

So if I really want to be smart and thin.
I'll have to get on with and just slim.

## Wishing

What's the use of wishing for the imaging pot of gold.
Beggars can't be choosers, least that's what I've been told.

So make the best of what God has given.
Remember, life is there just for the livin'.

He sends the rain to make the flowers grow.
We don't always appreciate it though I know.

The air we breathe is one of his many gifts.
Many things he sends help to give us all a lift.

Enjoy the things we have, count our many blessings.
A pity there has to be things that are so distressing.

He never promises we wouldn't find life hard.
So don't go chasing rainbows in someone else' back yard.

Try to keep cheerful helping others all we can.
Who knows just what can be achieved in one's life span.

## Small Beginnings

Share a smile, you never know what the outcome will be.
When next you're out smile at someone you will see.

Everything has small beginnings and I'm sure it's true.
A life-long friendship can start, with a just a smile from you.

A helping hand along the way, a cheery word when one is low.
Small things in themselves, but lifesavers sometimes you
know.

Wealth isn't always measured, by goods we have got.
It's the small unimportant things that really matter a lot.

Life's made up of small beginnings which grow as time goes
on.
So share a smile and spread some sunshine on this earth we
live upon.

## Mr. Wind's Many Moods

Mischievous Mr. Wind, he likes his little games.
Blowing people's hats off, at this he takes great pains.

Frolicking along, in a very playful mood.
Tugging at ladies' skirts, he's really quite rude.

But when he gets to gale force, that's when he shows his might.
Then playful mischief changes right round to spite.

Uprooting trees, and taking tiles off the roof.
Mr. Wind is in a temper, the sound gives us that proof.

Roaring down the chimney, whistling under the door.
Causing drafts, discomfort, and finding holes galore.

At sea he does untold damage, costs many, many lives.
Brave lifeboat mean to save them, heroically strive.

Fitting their puny strength against mountainous waves.
We give thanks to those gallant men, for every one they save.

Even on land Mr. Wind is a formidable force.
Showing his strength, and his temper of course.

Creating havoc and devastation, on a grand scale.
Spoiling all before him, leaving tragedy in his trail.

But we like him best, when on a warm sunny day.
He wafts the air to cool us, a lovely breeze we say.

## The Rescue

A crowd stood looking up at the old oak tree.
Clinging precariously, Mr. Jones' cat they could see.

His plaintive cries could be heard all around.
As if he was pleading with those on the ground.

A fireman, on his day off work, came along with his ladder.
But his efforts to reach the cat made him go higher.

Each time he raised his hand and reached out.
The frightened cat scratched him making him shout.

Up and up the cat went trying to flee.
Nearly to the top of that old oak tree.

Just out of reach, snarling and spitting.
The fireman all bruised with the branches he kept hitting.

When the branch he was on gave an ominous crack.
He thought, 'Cat or no cat I'd better get back.'

But as he tried, he found he was pinned.
He looked at the cat, and could have sown that it grinned.

Stuck on a branch, not a bit safe at all.
The crowd down below expected him to fall.

Very gently he freed himself and made his retreat.
Very thankful that he felt the ladder under his feet.

When he was once more safely on the ground.
He looked for the cat but it was nowhere to be found.

He had torn his trousers in a most conspicuous place.
With his hands spread out he rushed away with a very red
face.

Black cats are supposed to be lucky, so they say.
But that fireman didn't think they were, that particular day.

## The Snow Queen

The snow queen visits, never making a sound.
Silently, stealthily, covering the ground.

She plays havoc with traffic, makes workers late.
Forces motorists to abandon cars to their fate.

This mischievous lady, plays tricks on us.
Costs lots of money and creates a big fuss.

The chaos she causes, has to be seen.
Yet on a picture she is lovely, peaceful and serene.

With her image of loveliness, while still untouched.
But, not quite so lovely, when snow turns to slush.

Skiers on the slopes resemble birds in flight.
Flying down the mountains, they are a wondrous sight.

Children love her, making snowmen and slides.
Doing battles with snowballs, each taking sides.

Their laughter rings out as the missiles whiz past.
Reaching a crescendo as they fly thick and fast.

But the snow queen's enemy is Mr. Sun.
She soon fades away, when he joins in the fun.

# Tea

A pick me up it is said to be.
That grand old traditional cup of tea.

To wake us in a morning, we love our brew.
At regular intervals in the daytime we have one too.

It gives us a lift when we are feeling low.
It cheers us up with an inner glow.

Warms us up when the weather chills us thro.
Yet cools us down when the sun comes out too.

A cup of tea is the thought that enters the head.
When we hear bad news, which has to be said.

After shopping, the first thing we all seem to do.
Is sit down with a cuppa, well I do, don't you?

It it's a drug, then I'm addicted and don't mind at all.
It's a good think to offer when visitors come to call.

A pick me up in more ways than one.
Then relaxes us when the day is done.

Heavily sweetened it helps in cases of shock.
So as a lifesaver it's a remedy we shouldn't knock.

A way of life for us all it sure seems to be.
Where would we be, without our lovely cup of tea.

## A Helping Hand

When in the throes of dark deep despair.
It helps to know that there's someone there.

Someone how is always ready to understand.
Always glad to hold out a helping hand.

So take the help, don't turn it away.
Meet folks halfway, listen to what they say.

A hand held out in friendship, a token of goodwill.
There are lots who will help others up a steep hill.

Help your fellow travellers, it's manners to be kind.
Take the initiative; it works both ways you will find.

## Pigeons

Waiting for a bus in a bus station nearby.
I was watching some Pigeons flying up high.

Is it they, or us, who are confined?
Was the thought that idly passed thro my mind.

Wonder what they think as they survey.
The busy scene below, day by day.

Some folks laden with heavy shopping bags.
Others all dressed up in their glad rags.

While the Pigeons fly high and free as the air.
Wheeling about, with only the one care.

Their only worry what next to eat.
As they pick up tidbits from off the street.

Maybe we should take a leaf from their books.
And stop worrying how everything looks.

## The Predicament

Dolly a young girl, who was very accident prone.
Decided to have a bath while in the house alone.

She filled the bath up with lovely hot water.
Then uses the bath salts that some one had bought her.

Soaking in the tub, and nearly asleep.
She thought of the young man she was soon to meet.

The water went cool so she put up her foot.
To turn the tap on, but it was just her luck.

Her toe got stuck up the tap, and it wouldn't let go.
She pulled and she pulled at her big toe.

She'd heard of folks before in a similar pickle.
But up to now, thought it a bit of a giggle.

She tried and tried to free her toe, but it was stuck tight.
'Now don't panic,' she thought, 'it will be all right.'

She twisted this way and that, it really was a shame.
Nothing would work, so glared at the tap that was to blame.

Whatever could she do, it was getting quite late.
She would be stuck here forever, at this rate.

She shivered; the water was getting quite cold.
Her foot discoloured and swollen, a sight to behold.

She pulled out the plug, the gurgling water seemed to say.
'Dolly's got her toe stuck, and can't get away.'

Then she heard someone in the house next door.
So she knocked on the wall and banged on the floor.

She was getting cold and was feeling afraid.
'Please let someone come,' she silently prayed.

Eventually, someone answered her frantic plea.
She was past caring who it was so long as she got free.

That odious lad, she hated, burst in with a grin.
'Oh! Dear,' she thought, 'it would have to be him.'

He took in the situation at a glance, and to give him his due.
He did his best to help, but he hadn't a clue.

He tried this way and that, to get her toe free.
Accompanied by shouts of 'Oh you are hurting me.'

'I've a pal down the road, who will know what to do.
He's in the fire brigade, he'll be able to help you.'

Dolly said crossly, 'Fetch the marines as well.
Perhaps folk would pay for a peep, you never can tell.'

Off he went and Dolly was once more alone.
She couldn't help weeping and having a moan.

Soon they were back and they had brought some grease.
After a lot of fiddling, the toe they managed to release.

She sat in the bedroom with her foot on a stool.
Trying really hard not to feel such a fool.

Her foot would be sore for many a day.
To thank the two lads she didn't know what to say.

Dolly was so grateful, but she won out in the end.
As the fireman finished up as her special boy friend.

## Willie's Memorable Day Out

Willie went for a walk in the woods one day.
Enjoying the lovely weather as he went on his way.

Feeling tired he sat on a grassy bank, watching the sky.
Full of cotton wool cloud, drifting lazily by.

Very soon he grew sleepy, his head started to droop.
He dreamt he was in a plane, looping the loop.

Then he was riding on a great white horse.
Rescuing a damsel in distress of course.

He woke with a start and an anguished shout.
He had sat on an ants' nest, and the ants had come out.

'What shall I do' he thought in dismay.
Nothing he did, made them go away.

He twisted and squirmed like a fish on a hook.
He didn't have time to wonder how he must look.

The ants were biting and crawling all over him.
Then he had an idea, he would go for a swim.

Behind a big tree, he stripped to the skin.
Hoping to get all the ants off of him.

As he took off his clothes, he gave them a shake.
Then hung them on a tree branch for safety's sake.

There he stood naked, then giving a shiver.
Then bravely dived into the nearby river.

The ants all disappeared, the swim did the trick.
So he climbed out again, with the help of a stick.

But before he reached his clothes, he was startled to hear.
Ladies' voices oh help! They sounded quite near.

So behind a big tree he was forced to go.
Mustn't let them see him, oh dear me no!

His clothes he could see draped on the tree.
Right out in the open, where any one could see.

His hopes of them not being seen was dashed to the ground.
When he head a voice say, 'Hey, look what I've found.'

'They'll do for our Jumble sale, a tramp's left them here.'
Willie groaned as he sadly saw them disappear.

What a fix he was in, what ever could he do?
Standing there naked, and rapidly turning blue.

It was a local women's club out on a spree.
A picnic with a tablecloth and all, spread out for tea.

The one of the ladies cried, 'Come and look at this View.'
Willie nearly died, well, wouldn't you too?

They all wandered off, leaving one lady behind.
Willie's thoughts, just then, were anything but kind.

When her back was turned, he leaned over with his stick.
And deftly hooked the tablecloth with a twist and a flick.

Then he wrapped it around his middle as best he could.
At least he was covered, now he must get out of the wood.

Hoping against hope that no one he would see.
While flitting foot sore and weary, from tree to tree.

Covered in ant bites, he felt such an ass.
He vowed never again would he sit on the grass.

But he thought he had better wait until it was dark.
Before even daring to sneak home through the park.

He did hear later, Dai Jones had signed the pledge.
On seeing one night, by a ghost gliding through a hedge.

So be warned, don't sit on an ants' nest what ever you do.
Or maybe the same sort of thing could happen to you.

## Winter

Red noses, tingling fingers and toes.
Are a part of December, for that's how it goes.

Jack Frost is here; he's been busy again.
Painting dainty feathery patterns on the window pane.

Slippery icy paths making children squeal with delight.
While older people view them with horror and fright.

Woollies come out when the north wind doth blow.
That's when the saying says we will have snow.

Shoppers battling against bleak wintry weather.
Rush to get home, being inside is a pleasure.

Curtains are drawn to shut out the dark night.
A cosy fire becomes a scene of delight.

Gaily decorated shops foster the Christmas spirt.
December heralds winter, and all that goes with it.

## Peace

P stands for Patience, a thing the world sadly lacks.
E is for Emotion, a feeling everyone attacks.

A stands for Anger; which should be kept in check.
C is for Calmness, anger can soon wreck.

E is for if Every one in this old world really believed.
Peace in this world could perhaps be achieved.

Peace and prosperity, friendship one man with another.
Who was it said, 'Treat every man just like a brother'?

www.ingramcontent.com/pod-product-compliance
Lightning Source LLC
Chambersburg PA
CBHW071937020426
42331CB00010B/2905